How to Defeat the New World Order

By

Rick Thomas

How to Defeat the New World Order

"There seems to be nothing to prevent the transnational corporations taking possession of the planet and subjecting humanity to the dictatorship of capital….In order to crush any thought of organized resistance to the supporters of the new world order, tremendous police and military forces are being used to establish a doctrine of repression…"

~ French newspaper Le Monde Diplomatique May 1999

"The Plan is for the United States to rule the world. The overt theme is unilateralism, but it is ultimately a story of domination. It calls for the United States to maintain its overwhelming superiority and prevent new rivals from rising up to challenge it on the world stage. It calls for dominion over friends and enemies alike. It says not that the United States must be more powerful, or most powerful, but that it must be absolutely powerful."

~ US Vice President Dick Cheney, June 2002

"International order is created by force, preserved by force and backed by the threat of force…questions about whether it is legal or not seem, at this stage in world history, at least, merely pedantic."

~ Tony Blair's diplomatic representative Robert Cooper, New Statesman, September 9 2002

"If democracy is ever to be threatened, it will not be by revolutionary groups burning government offices and occupying the broadcasting and newspaper offices of the world. It will come from disenchantment, cynicism and despair caused by the realization that the New World Order, means we are all to be managed and not represented."

~ British MP Tony Benn

"The New World Order cannot happen without U.S. participation, as we are the single most significant component. Yes, there will be a New World Order, and it will force the United States to change its perception."

~ Henry Kissinger 1994

"Finally, history has shown that all opposition to entrenched oligarchy arises from the middle classes, who have the surplus of funds needed to challenge the ruling classes. The New World Order will have to, indeed already is, following the same model. If the general population only has enough to pay for the next day's rent and food, they will do as they are told."

~ Michael Rivero

"There is no such thing as the United Nations. There is an international community that can be led by the only real power left in the world, and that is the US, when it suits our interests and when we can get others to go along."

~ US Ambassador to the UN John Bolton

Contents

CHAPTER ONE

HOW DID THIS HAPPEN?

A terrible war has been unleashed on the world, a war unlike any other. This is an unprecedented assault on humanity and therefore it requires an unprecedented response. We need to come together and unite like never before. The conventional concepts of protests, activism, demonstrations and marches that have worked in the past may require a new strategy for this particular crisis. This book is an effort to look at strategies that are proven effective that will guarantee our victory for future generations.

The marches and rallies of 2020 did not topple any governments anywhere despite the fact that protests in Berlin and London in August numbered in the hundreds of thousands; some estimates put the Berlin protest over one million. Protests in these record numbers should have resulted in the overthrow of the government under normal circumstances but these are not normal circumstances. The truth is nothing happened. The health orders did not change nor were restrictions lifted.

What do we need to do differently? First of all, we need to start with a better question: How did we get here? A brief review of the last century reveals that the two world wars and the endless series of minor and major conflicts between nations resulted in 200 million dead. The last twenty years of the so-called "war-on-terror" have resulted in military operations in Afghanistan, Pakistan, Baluchistan, Mali, Somalia, Philippines, Yemen, Syria, Libya and Cameroon. According to the Watson Institute the War-on-Terror cost the United States over $6 trillion and 800,000 people have died as a direct result of the violence of these conflicts; nearly 38 million people have been displaced or made refugees. If these were the only problems in the world today it would still be a horrific tragedy but our modern societies have also produced escalating divorce rates, suicides, drug and alcohol addiction, mental illness, homelessness and depression.

Civil unrest, rioting and demonstrations are occurring all over the world at an unprecedented rate; despite the global shutdown of economies and stay-at-home orders the world experienced 230 large-scale anti-government protests that occurred in 110 countries in 2020.

Combined with this is the ever-increasing wealth inequality that has seen the upper 1% of human society owning 80% of the world's wealth. Western billionaires Jeff Bezos, Elon Musk and Bill Gates increased their fortunes by billions of dollars while the average person was unemployed, stressed out, depressed and fearful; being forced to stay home and mask up or face fines and imprisonment. Walmart had a record year in 2020 as sales were up 74%.

But how did we get in this mess?

The short version is something like this: The Enlightenment thinkers of the 1700's rebelled against the totalitarian medieval church who dominated European society. This rebellion and fight for human rights and equality was the catalyst for the American, French,

Russian and Chinese Revolutions. It also instigated the scientific revolution that is still racing down the tracks like a locomotive without any brakes.

However, the Enlightenment thinkers like Voltaire, Rousseau and Diderot went too far and not only did they rebel against the Church but they also instigated a revolt against God, Christianity and any form of spirituality or religion.

"This confirms all that I have said of the Enlighterners, very aptly called Philosophists; and of the abuses of Freemasonry in France. It shows, unquestionably, that a formal systematic conspiracy against Religion was formed and zealously prosecuted by Voltaire, d-Alembert and Diderot, assisted by Frederick II, King of Prussia; and I see that their principles and their manner of procedure have been the same with those of the German atheists and anarchists."

~ John Robison, Proofs of a Conspiracy Against All the Religions and Governments of Europe, 1798

The world has never known a time without religion. Every society has always had some kind of belief, whether it was paganism, animism, polytheism, ancestor worship or monotheism. Human beings have always believed in something higher than themselves; the belief in an afterlife is universal in human history up until the last two or three hundred years.

In early ancient Greek, the adjective *átheos* meant "godless." It was first used as a term of censure roughly meaning "ungodly" or "impious." In the 5th century BC, the word began to indicate more deliberate and active godlessness in the sense of "severing relations with the gods" or "denying the gods."

Western nations in particular and modern nations all over the world, in Asia, Africa, South America and elsewhere have departed from the traditional belief in a higher power. Modern men and women don't think they need God, religion or spirituality.

Materialism, secularism, humanism and atheism promote the idea that the universe is a self-created, accidental fluke without any purpose, meaning or direction; they claim we have no spiritual parent or creator and life is only mortal, temporary and fleeting.

Global Distribution of Wealth

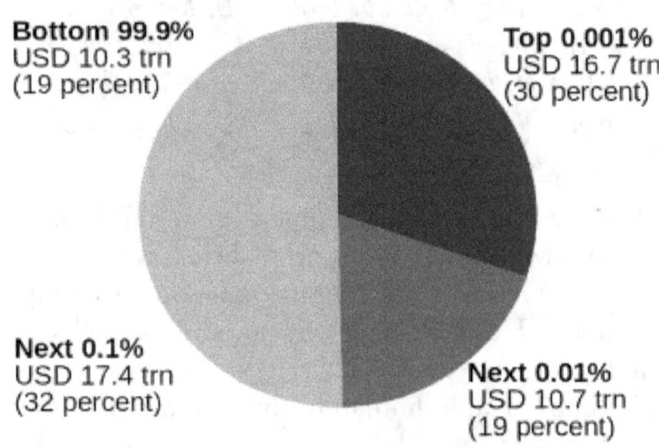

There is no denying the advances science and technology have given the modern world. Life expectancy has doubled in the last one hundred years and overall improvements have produced a much better world in so many ways but even *the best laid plans of mice and men often go astray*; this scientific age has also produced the unwanted harvest of civil unrest, human misery and world wars.

Improvements due to innovation in science and technology have moved the world many steps forward but these same advances in technology are now threatening to enslave the whole human race in an unprecedented assault on all our hard-fought-for freedoms.

"There's class warfare, all right, but it's my class, the rich class, that's making war, and we're winning."

~ US billionaire Warren Buffett.

Wealth inequality is not the cause of our modern problems – it's a symptom. The root cause of our modern problems is human greed, selfishness, power-lust, war madness and the sociopathic inbreeding of aristocratic degenerates. When a society is spiritually healthy and family relationships are strong, the sociopaths are unable to rise to the top because the good people are in positions of power and responsibility. The saying that *the only condition for evil to flourish is good people do nothing* may be a cliché but it is nonetheless true.

When the Enlightenment philosophers, technocrats and intellectuals abandoned God, it created a power vacuum that sociopathic men and women were only too happy and eager to fill. These men and women with little or no conscience entrenched themselves in positions of power and created the worst totalitarian regimes in history. Hitler, Stalin and Mao were all atheists. Stalin instituted *The League of Militant Atheists* who went on a decade-long rampage on Christians and Muslims, killing thousands of priests and sending millions to the Gulags.

The Russian Revolution of March 1917 was originally a populist movement of peasants and industrial textile workers who protested on the streets demanding bread because the commoners were starving due to the war fought against Germany. The peasant farmers wanted land of their own; they were tired of being feudal serfs to landowners; the general population wanted Russia out of World War I which was bankrupting the nation and causing the deaths of thousands of soldiers.

The people, especially women made great gains in equal rights, land ownership and improved working conditions but sadly the Bolsheviks co-opted the revolution and staged a coup in November of 1917 and plunged Russian into 62 years of totalitarian communism; first under Lenin and than an even worse tyrant Joseph Stalin who reversed most of the gains in civil rights and freedoms.

In France, the French Revolution freed the French people from the clutches of the Church and the church-controlled monarchy but soon after the people were sold into slavery by the Napoleonic military machine that ravaged Europe with a dozen years of wars killing 4.3 million soldiers and civilians. Out of the frying pan and into the fire.

The truth is we need spirituality and religion despite the flaws and inconsistency of religious organizations and despite the differences and contradictions of different faiths. Muslim, Buddhist, Christian, New Age, Native, Hindu and all the other ways of approaching faith and belief are valid paths that are informed by the inner divine spark, the still small voice that leads and guides us ever onward and upward. We are all brothers and sisters, part of a world-wide universal family parented by the great source and center, father, creator, Great Spirit of all creation.

CHAPTER TWO

KNOW YOUR ENEMY

There can be no victory over any enemy whether human, biological, animal or vegetable without first understanding the character, motivation, agenda and methods of the enemy. Failure to study and examine the inner motives, plans and goals of the men and women who are currently working night and day to enslave all of humanity is courting disaster for all of those fighting to win this most epic battle in all human history.

Shrewd, wicked and scheming men ought never to be allowed in any position of responsibility but here we are today with a cult of 600 billionaire families who have entrenched themselves in positions of power and they rule most of the world.

The American Empire

"Never before in history has one nation had more power over more people in more spheres of life than does the United States."

~ Nicaraguan Representative to the UN, Alejandro Bendana.

A distinction has to be made between America the Nation and America the Empire. The elites control both, and although America is their base of operations, the political cult we are discussing are not all Americans but rather they are a wide assortment of the ruling class of America, Britain, Canada, Europe, Israel and the rest of the Nato/ G20 nations. For the purposes of this brief book, we will call the elites the *Empire.*

America the Nation is just one province or fiefdom in the overall empire. The president is only a frontman for the nation of America and doesn't represent the whole Empire though he does its bidding. Current presidents read prepared speeches from teleprompters and make few if any policy decisions on the international stage. They are directed by their controllers and handlers, primarily the Council on Foreign Relations.

The Empire is a political cult or political party similar to other political groups except for a few distinctions. One is their emphasis on secrecy. The men at the top prefer to remain anonymous and stay out of the media. You will rarely hear their names mentioned. The billionaires and politicians we see on the media are the front men and women who act as their public relations officers and propagandists.

To the best of my knowledge, Henry Kissinger is the CEO and mastermind behind this cult since at least the 1960's. Kissinger is a political genius, albeit an evil genius. He doesn't have many years left so my guess is his successor is possibly Bill Gates, Klaus Schwab or Mike Bloomberg, though none of them are as politically savvy as Dr. K.

The Empire is run by a council of 300 men who are dominated by 25 men at the top. Your guess is as good as mine as to the identity of these men but most of us in the movement are fairly certain of the names of many of them. They act as the board of directors for the cult. They are corporate men. They want ORDER above all else; a top-down highly authoritarian, highly efficient, technologically-managed machine. They attend meetings,

meetings and more meetings and like all corporate organizations there are endless power point presentations with graphs and maps and strategies. They are everything a hippie is not.

Like all totalitarian regimes, they are heavily dependent on bureaucracy. The spirituality of a society is inversely proportional to the level of bureaucracy. They despise freewill in human beings and one of their main goals is to stamp out and forever destroy the freewill of human beings. Too bad for them their psychotic dreams will never be realized. These men and their plans are doomed, in every sense of the word.

The Nazis and the Soviets are two examples from history of totalitarian cults that are instructive in understanding how our enemy is different from any other previous political organization. The Nazis were a political party who were elected democratically through the legal, political process in Germany. They gained their authority through a mandate from the people.

The Bolsheviks rose to power through an armed coup of the Provisional Government set up by their political enemies. They engaged in a coup followed by a lengthy and bloody civil war to retain and consolidate their power. They fought openly and debated in public with their political enemies, slandering and murdering each other for control of Soviet Russia. The real losers were the peasants and working class who were no better off than they were before under the Tsarist Romanov family.

The difference with the Empire is that it has come into power through covert means. The Nazis and the Soviets after coming into power created secret service agencies and police units like the Gestapo and the Okhrana who systematically oppressed, imprisoned and murdered their enemies. The Empire has done the opposite. It is a secret intelligence agency that has infiltrated all levels of society and it operates primarily through the CIA and its affiliates, Mossad, MI6, CSIS and the other Five Eyes of Australia and New Zealand. The other sixteen US intelligence agencies such as the NSA are involved at the highest levels.

"The New World Order will have to be built from the bottom up rather than from the top down…run around national sovereignty, eroding it piece by piece will accomplish much more than the old-fashioned frontal assault."

~ Richard Gardner, US Council on Foreign Relations Journal Foreign Affairs, April 1974.

The Empire sets up think tanks and front organizations such as the Trilateral Commission, the Council on Foreign Relations, Chatham House, Canadian Institute of International Affairs and the more recent Quadrilateral Security Dialogue (QSD, also known as the Quad.) Other well-known groups are the Davos World Economic Forum and the Bilderberg Club who meet every year to discuss and manage the ongoing plans and policies of the Empire.

"The Trilateral Commission is intended to be the vehicle for multinational consolidation of the commercial and banking interests by seizing control of the political government of the United States. The Trilateral Commission represents a skillful, coordinated effort to seize control and consolidate the four centers of power political, monetary, intellectual and ecclesiastical. What the Trilateral Commission intends is to create a worldwide economic power superior

to the political governments of the nation states involved. As managers and creators of the system, they will rule the future."

~ *US Senator Barry Goldwater.*

These think tanks are funded, staffed and managed by the Empire to further the goal of establishing a global totalitarian state run by them. With their wealth, power and influence they have built up over the decades a coalition of willing agents who are rewarded with high-paying positions of influence and prestige in our societies. There are many, many other groups, fraternities, secret societies, NGO's and organizations that are part of the Empire's power base. Without a doubt, this is the most powerful political cult in history and we should never under-estimate them.

"Power is not a means; it is an end. One does not establish a dictatorship in order to safeguard a revolution; one makes the revolution in order to establish the dictatorship. The object of persecution is persecution. The object of torture is torture. The object of power is power."

~ *George Orwell, 1984*

One thing that is very difficult to understand for normal, decent people is the motivation of this political cult. It's hard to understand that some people enjoy killing people, causing suffering, torturing children and causing human misery. Power is the ultimate drug for these sociopathic men and women. They get an ego woody that sends a rush of adrenaline into their brains whenever they exercise their power over others. It's one of the reason it's very difficult to convince our poor lost sheep brothers and sisters that this is what is happening. They just can't go there.

Fabian Strategy

"This type of strategy is named for a Roman General. In this strategy you avoid a direct, frontal assault and instead you gradually wear down your opponent over time using indirect attacks. This type of military strategy was used by General Washington to defeat the British, by the Russians to defeat Napoleon and by Sam Houston to defeat Santa Anna. This strategy works only in situations where you have time on your side and the discipline to maintain a continual attack which slowly weakens your opponent. It has also been used in nonmilitary situations. Corporations sometimes use such approaches to defeat competitors. The British Fabian Society is attempting to use this type of strategy to promote their socialist agenda. The Illuminati itself is attempting to use a Fabian Strategy to conquer the world."

~ Fabian Therapy for Mind Control

You can observe their strategy right now as the Empire is incrementally pushing their agenda from many fronts; using the media, the governments and the medical profession to advance their assault on humanity. The leaders remain invisible so it's very difficult to see the source of their attacks. They create a lot of smoke and mirrors to hide their movements. The pandemic is in reality just smoke and mirrors to enable them to crash the economy and bring in their new technology while the whole world is distracted and preoccupied with the Covid-19 melodrama. It's a live-action reality TV show.

The Fabian Society named themselves after this strategy and called it the "doctrine of inevitability of gradualism," which meant that their goals would be gradually achieved. So gradual, that nobody would notice, or "without breach of continuity or abrupt change of the entire social issue." They are using slow evolution, not revolution, or as many people have commented: a frog in a pot of slowly boiling water.

This Isn't Communism

One thing that should be pointed out is that their goal isn't communism, contrary to the opinion of many conservatives. They want a corporate-style board of directors over each nation and a similar board of unelected, hereditary managers who will rule the world with an iron fist through technology like Artificial Intelligence, surveillance and data-mining.

The Empire is first and foremost a group of *monopoly capitalists*. These men and women became billionaires by destroying their competition and monopolizing markets; men like John D. Rockefeller is a perfect example of a monopolist who ruthlessly exploited and crushed his competition to corner the oil market. Bill Gates is another example of a billionaire who systematically destroyed the competition and cornered the PC market; now he is repeating it with the pharmaceutical industry.

The plans of the elites bear one similarity with Marxist communist ideas and that is the abolition of private property. The Great Reset promoted by Klaus Schwab and the World Economic Forum (WEF) is however advocating more than abolition of private property; they are also suggesting we have no *personal property* and people will just rent their possessions.

Marx advocated state controlled means of production but what the WEF is promoting is *corporate* controlled means of production. The workers of the world will not control anything nor is the WEF advocating a worker's revolution. What they are advocating is a universal basic income where we would pay no taxes but we would be slaves to the corporate state. In contrast to Marx who suggest there should a graduated tax system.

Marxism also promoted equality of men and women and it is largely due to the communist women such as in Russia where the communists first introduced women's suffrage in 1917. Schwab and his psychopath pals are pushing for a genderless society where no one has any rights at all and elections would be abolished.

Another difference is that universal healthcare which is a plank of the communist platform is not being promoted by the Empire. Although this is a medical tyranny we are currently experiencing, the only universal treatment they are proscribing is vaccines.

What the Empire wants is a corporate feudal state run by corporate monopoly capitalists who own everything. Marx was completely opposed to capitalism so it could not be said that the Empire members are communists. What the Empire wants is far worse than anything communists like Stalin or Mao ever instituted. They want *governance* not government.

CHAPTER THREE

SOCIOPATHS

You will know them by their fruits. Are grapes gathered from thorns, or figs from thistles? So, every sound tree bears good fruit, but the bad tree bears evil fruit. A sound tree cannot bear evil fruit, nor can a bad tree bear good fruit.

~ Jesus of Nazareth

There has been much study in recent years about sociopaths to try and understand who and what they are; and a definite pattern has emerged that reveals the similarities in behavior of evil men and women.

A Conscience Seared

The most striking quality of a sociopath is the complete lack of remorse over wrongdoing. They have no conscience and feel no guilt for their actions, no matter how immoral. They lack empathy and emotional reaction to people and events; most are incapable of love or compassion; for them, people are just objects to be used or opponents to be defeated.

Robert D. Hare, one of the foremost experts on sociopaths states, "Completely lacking in conscience and in feelings for others, they selfishly take what they want and do as they please, violating social norms and expectations without the slightest sense of guilt or regret."

Sociopaths consistently reveal a total lack of conscience. They seem to have no remorse or feelings of guilt about their crimes or evil behavior. They are consummate actors who learn to imitate normal social behavior and pretend to be interested in people but in reality they are only interested like a predator is interested in its prey.

According to Andrzej Łobaczewski, who pioneered the study of political sociopaths, "Natural human reactions… strike the sociopath as strange, interesting, and even comical. They therefore observe us…they become experts in our weaknesses and sometimes effect heartless experiments."

They have no empathy towards others and their outward personality is a carefully studied portrait that they spend years learning to project. According to Sam Vaknin, who is a self-confessed sociopath, "Most sociopaths are subtle, more like poison than a knife, and more like slow-working poison."

Most have no emotional life; they are like a shark whose sole purpose is eating. They present a visage of modesty and humanity: they are imitators of good behavior; and successful sociopaths are often more convincing than ordinary people. And by successful, that usually means someone who has advanced in corporate, political or financial areas. Criminals are considered by some researchers to be "unsuccessful sociopaths."

Wear Mask

A sociopath imitates the behavior of normal people; he or she studies how people react and exhibit emotion and works hard at mastering these behaviors. Emotional reactions to situations result from the presence of a conscience and because sociopaths do not have a conscience, they can only pretend to be normal. Successful sociopaths are known to be outwardly charming and personable; they have a knack for knowing what people want to hear.

"Sociopaths are social predators who charm, manipulate, and ruthlessly plow their way through life, leaving a broad trail of broken hearts, shattered expectations, and empty wallets," say Robert D. Hare the Canadian psychologist who devised the Hare sociopathy Checklist (PCL) which is commonly used today to evaluate sociopathic behavior.

Their outward personality is a carefully studied portrait that they spend years learning to project. They are usually good talkers and very good at lying. They all lie, often for fun, are aware they are lying and indifferent to the truth; when caught lying they make up more lies.

Bill Gates is a prime example of someone who re-invented and rebranded himself, donning pastel sweaters and assuming a nerdier voice; he also dumped billions into his the Bill and Melinda Gates foundation which is a tax-free piggy bank to fund his so-called philanthropy. This is nothing new for cult members of the Empire to rebrand themselves as humanitarians after spending decades ruthlessly exploiting humanity.

Godless

They are also atheistic, or at the very least, indifferent to religion, spirituality or God. The greatest mass-murderers of the last century, Stalin, Mao, Pol Pot and Hitler were all atheists who murdered believers in the millions. Hitler, who acknowledged a vague belief in what he called Providence, publicly maintained he was a Christian but in private he hated religion. Joseph Goebbels wrote in 1941 that Hitler "hates Christianity, because it has crippled all that is noble in humanity."

Sociopaths may use religion as a cover to appear normal, upright and respectable or they may infiltrate a religious group to take advantage of its members. It is highly likely that some high-profile religious leaders are sociopaths because they are enormously attracted to power and wealth. There are numerous religious leaders who have amassed significant wealth and have influence over millions of people.

Stalin's own daughter Svetlana had this to say about her deranged father's final moments on his death bed:

> "The death agony was terrible. God grants an easy death only to the just. He literally choked to death as we watched. At what seemed like the very last moment he suddenly opened his eyes and cast a glance over everyone in the room. It was a terrible glance, insane or perhaps angry and full of fear of death…Then something incomprehensible and terrible happened that to this day I can't forget… He suddenly lifted his left hand as though he were pointing to something up above and bring down a curse on us all. The gesture was incomprehensible and full of menace…The next moment, after a final effort, the spirit wrenched itself free of the flesh."

Hypnotic Eyes

One remarkable trait that sociopaths share is their penetrating eyes. Often dazzling or shining, those close to sociopaths describe their eyes as hypnotic, piercing and seem to look right through people into their soul. Researchers often comment on their "reptilian stare" and note their ability to maintain intense eye contact with people.

Adolf Hitler was known for his hypnotic eyes – women were mostly afraid of him because of his penetrating gaze. Robert Waite writes in his book *Adolf Hitler: The Sociopathic God:*

> "The most impressive feature of his otherwise coarse and rather undistinguished face was his eyes. They were extraordinarily light blue in color, with a faint touch of greenish-gray. Almost everyone who met him mentioned his strangely compelling eyes. This includes the German dramatist Gerhart Hauptmann who, when first introduced to Hitler, stared into his famous eyes and later told friends, 'It was the greatest moment of my life!'"

James Clarke in *Last Rampage*, a biography of killer Gary Tison who went on a shooting spree while escaping from prison and murdered a family of four, describes him in a similar fashion:

> "But Gary's most striking physical feature – the thing most people noticed and never forgot – was his deep-set, expressionless eyes. It was as if his eyes had no connection with any emotion he expressed. Whatever his mood – whether he was angry, jovial, or anything in between – his eyes remained the same. Empty. It was impossible to tell what Gary was actually thinking or feeling looking at his eyes...His stare was riveting, unsettling, with a malign intensity. What people remembered most about Gary were those cold, hard eyes."

Childhood

Even from birth the wicked go astray; from the womb they are wayward, spreading lies.

~ Psalm 58:3

Sociopaths invariably reveal themselves from a very young age and usually start exhibiting behavioral problems by age 10 to 12. Things like chronic lying, cheating, theft, fire setting, truancy, class disruption, substance abuse, vandalism, violence, bullying, running away, early promiscuity and cruelty to animals are common to most sociopaths. They are also often cruel to other children, including siblings.

In 1966, the psychiatry researcher Lee Robins conducted a series of studies on children with behavioral problems, following them into adulthood. In her book, *Deviant Children Grown Up*, she showed that those studies revealed that nearly every sociopathic adult was deeply antisocial as a child.

The evidence suggested that it mattered little whether a child was raised in a good family or an abusive one. This led many researchers to conclude that the answer must be genetic or organic, that sociopaths were predisposed due to some mutation in their genes or they were suffering from some disease of the brain akin to schizophrenia.

The obvious conclusion that most professionals in the field seem reluctant to admit is that evil is a choice that even very young children can make from their earliest days. We are freewill creatures and that means we can choose good or evil.

The thing that is very difficult to understand is that sociopaths enjoy inflicting pain and suffering on others. Sadistic people get supreme satisfaction when they have power and control over others. It gives their egos the ultimate glory high that becomes an addictive drug over time when repeated continually.

Money gives the Empire power. Power is what they crave, not money. The feeling of godliness and exaltation when they are able to manipulate whole groups of people and even entire nations is exhilarating for them. They can start wars and bankrupt people and companies, steer media in any direction they want.

There is a reason the sociopaths and their agents who run the Empire have a chessboard of black and white squares as one of their key symbols. Life is just a giant chess game to them and they only play to win. They move the pieces around the board, pitting one side against the other but it doesn't matter which side wins or loses, they still come out ahead and further their agenda.

Lexington Lodge No. 1 Freemasons The Oldest Masonic Lodge in Kentucky. Chartered in 1788

CHAPTER FOUR

PSYCHOLOGICAL WARFARE

Conventional wars of the past have been fought between armed combatants with guns, tanks, airplanes and ships. Other means such as chemical and biological warfare have also been used during times of war. Propaganda wars were conducted between the various Allied and Axis powers in the second world war using radio and newsprint. The Nazis utilized propaganda to a greater extent than anyone previously and it was Joseph Goebbels who fully utilized film as a propaganda tool.

The Chinese philosopher Sun Tzu said, *All war is based on deception.* Previous wars have used propaganda, media and psychological warfare only as an addition to their bag of tricks but this current war is completely based on the deceptions of the media and medical profession. The Empire has chosen to abandon overt means in favor of covert means. This also give them plausible deniability.

Lies in the media can always be backed up with more lies. Science can be manipulated by paid liars, many of the scientists, doctors and professionals have been bribed, coerced, threatened or offered advancement in the Empire. The use of green screens, CGI and many sophisticated tools of media manipulation makes it possible to create any story necessary to convince a gullible and naive population anything the Empire wants the people to believe.

You can fool some of the sheep some of the time but you can't fool all of the sheep all of the time. The mass political awakening since the events of 9/11 has only increased because of the plandemic of 2020.

The word *psyche* is from the Greek and it literally means *soul.* Psychological abuse and torture of entire populations are managed by forcing people to stay isolated and unemployed, cooped up in their homes like delinquent children who are grounded by their parents. Except that adults who are under financial stress resort to alcohol and drug abuse. Domestic abuse soon follows.

Prisons use solitary confinement as a punishment. Aloneness creates a sense of hopelessness and it is psychologically deflating. Human beings wilt without their brothers and sisters, family and friends.

Mass Hypnosis

We've never been so saturated and bombarded with media like we are now. Television, cable TV, Netflix, porn, radio, social media, video games and a multitude of chat groups and text messaging have exploded in the last twenty years. Cell phones have made it possible for the average person, rich or poor, to be in constant and continual communication with social media. Data mining professionals have become experts at feeding populations information and more importantly for the Empire, censoring information that doesn't fit their current version of reality.

Human beings are extremely sensitive to voice commands and suggestions from authority figures. Since our childhood we have been trained to conform to our society's social demands through our parents and education systems. The teacher is the first authority figure children encounter in an institutional setting and it is engrained in us to behave, sit still, do our work, keep quiet and pay attention to the authority figure.

Television, news and media present us with daily authority figures that remind, reassure and re-educate the population every single day with a series of narratives about our countries, communities and institutions. The reference to "experts" is reinforced on a daily basis; we are constantly told by our supposed betters how to view events, people and groups. Science is used as a weapon to control public opinion and steer the narrative in certain directions.

Propaganda and mass hypnosis are achieved by the constant repetition of key phrases and symbols. The current psychological operation uses the phrases:

stay home, social distancing, self-isolation, stay 6 feet apart, wear a mask, wash your hands

These phrases are reinforced by simple symbols that have appeared absolutely everywhere in the last year. The main ingredient to make this all work properly is *fear.*

De-programming

People in our society, in fact the whole world is suffering from mass hypnosis, mind control and media manipulation. The world is being brainwashed like a religious cult brainwashes its members. Cults use simple techniques of programming like depriving new converts of food, water and sleep. Isolation and fear accomplishes everything. Trauma-based mind control is the fastest way to inculcate a helpless population to accept new ideas and instructions.

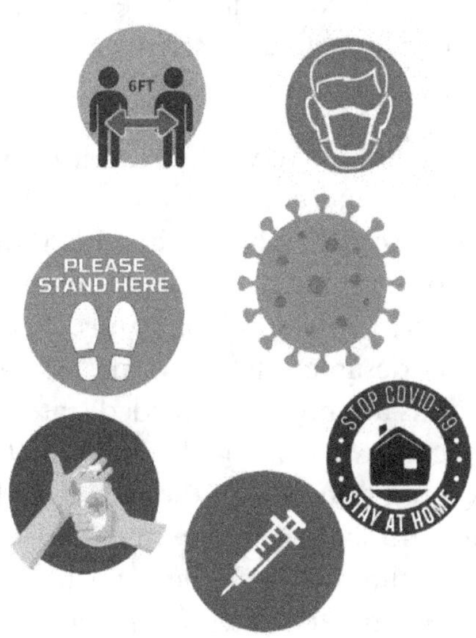

A person or a society who is in shock, afraid, depressed and isolated is easy pickings for the media agencies of the Empire to prey upon. The major corporations who have such enormous control over our societies are the second wing of this psychological warfare. The symbol of a face wearing a mask is plastered all over the entire world. Every store, business and residence is required to have these symbols and they are also required to enforce the wearing of masks inside any indoor space.

What the media has created is essentially a pseudo-scientific medical cult with appropriate symbols and slogans. The high priests are people like Dr. Fauci, Bill Gates, Dr. Tedros of the W.H.O., Health officers Teresa

Tam, Bonnie Henry and UK Health Minister Matt Hancock. The words and orders of these so-called experts are like a magic spell uttered by a shaman. They are not to be questioned or contradicted because they have the divine authority of the gods of science.

Mind Control

The same techniques that the Empire uses in their experiments with mind control with individuals are being used on a mass scale. "The victims of Illuminati mind control are programmed with commands that are implanted into their subconscious minds. These implanted commands are designed to keep them under control. These commands are precisely worded statements that are given to the victim when he or she is in an altered state of mind. This altered state makes the victim highly receptive to suggestion. Implanted commands are given which instruct the victim so that he or she is unable to consciously remember having been programmed." [Fabian Therapy for Mind Control.]

While our whole world is distraught, frightened and traumatized by the Covid-19 terror attack, the media introduces and implants new concepts and instructions to change the behavior and direction of all human society.

The same Fabian Strategy that is being used to program and conquer the world can also be used to de-program and reverse the direction of the world by avoiding direct confrontation and using an indirect, more subtle approach over a long period of time.

"The basic process of all Illuminati mind control is to create a blank slate so that the programmer can write whatever he wants to on it." This same technique is used on a massive scale with the whole world. Part of their plans is to remove our current culture, music, worship, recreation and leisure and therefore create a blank slate to insert the new social program.

The ultimate goal of the Empire's mind control is to develop a psychiatric technology for destroying free will in humans.

How to Deprogram the Lost Sheep

In the 1970's there were a plethora of religious cults that mushroomed all over North America and Europe. Parents of young people hired cult de-programmers and paid them thousands of dollars to kidnap and detain their kids and forcibly de-program them. Some of their methods were brutal: they beat and tortured the helpless cult members and forced them to become de-programmed; some charged fees of $25,000. Today's de-programmers are called "exit counselors" and they are more humane.

1. The most essential thing in our efforts to deprogram the poor lost sheep who have been brainwashed by media is to first convince them they are in fact programmed and brainwashed.

2. The programmed person first needs to be open to having a conversation without getting into aggressive debate. Don't waste your time on hostile people. Don't throw your pearls to swine.

3. Discuss the motivation of the Empire. When a crime is committed the question to ask is always *Who Benefits?* Show them how Big Pharma, Bill Gates, the billionaires and corporations have benefited most from this plandemic.

4. Reason with them, don't argue and debate.

5. Plant seeds. Don't expect them to turn on a dime with one meeting. Conversion requires conversation. Lots of conversation. Just leave them with some ideas and let them go. They will think about it all later. Give them time to digest and do some follow up research on their own.

6. Testimonials are helpful. "I used to be a sheep just like you" is powerful. Nobody can argue with personal experience. Share your story.

7. Identify and disprove myths. Example: "Vaccines have never hurt anyone."

8. Show history of disinfo and lies. Unless you have a very good memory for details like this, you will probably have to send them links and more info later.

9. Most important is respect and compassion. Always remember they are not the enemy and we should treat everyone as if they are already on our side, they just need more time and info so be patient.

CHAPTER FIVE

GIVE THE ENEMY WHAT IT DOESN'T WANT

One of the main principles of warfare is to find out what the enemy doesn't want you to do and then go out and do it. Fortunately for us, the enemy has spent an entire year telling us openly what they don't want us to do. As we mentioned earlier, the Empire has created a medical health cult with symbols and slogans. They've also created a list of Thou-Shalt-Nots written not in stone but written in the media and plastered over front doors of businesses everywhere.

Here's the 10 Commandments of the Covid Cult:

1. Thou shalt not go out of the house without permission

2. Thou shalt not go out without a mask

3. Thou shalt not hug or touch each other

4. Thou shalt not get within 6 feet of each other

5. Thou shalt not have parties or events with friends and family

6. Thou shalt not worship together

7. Thou shalt not sing or dance or make music

8. Thou shalt not take any medicine, supplement or treatment except vaccines

9. Thou shalt not protest or march

10. Thou shalt not promote any medical science except the cult medical science

The reason why the Empire has been so successful in making these 10 Commandments work is that they have completely brainwashed the public into believing these commandments will save our souls from the deadly sin of the virus. Like a religious cult, they have made us all sinners who are unclean and defiled. We must all be purified by the salvation of the vaccine that will take away the sinful virus and redeem us all.

The vaccine is communion for the brainwashed sheep. They take it in the hopes it will absolve them of all their sins of contagion and infection. Like the lepers in ancient times, the unvaccinated and unclean will be forced out of the towns and cities and made to live in camps. Interesting to note in Leviticus we find this about the lepers:

"Anyone with such a defiling disease must wear torn clothes, let their hair be unkempt, cover the lower part of their face [wear a mask] and cry out, 'Unclean! Unclean!' As long as they have the disease they remain unclean. They must live alone; they must live outside the camp."

~Leviticus 13:45-46

Once the unclean have been vaccinated they receive the blessings of the high priests Fauci and Gates. Our health ministers and officials are the bishops and cardinals. Bill Gates is the pope of this cult organization controlled by the W.H.O., the John Hopkins University and the Rockefeller Foundation who provide the funding and the strategy.

The world is depressed and traumatized. They need our compassion and our real kindness, not the fake kindness offered by our sociopathic medical overlords. Our health minister here in British Columbia is a poster girl for the whole cult, the Covid Mother Teresa who always says the magic words: *Be Kind, Be Calm, Be Safe* is her trademark slogan. One of the main reasons why British Columbia is so passive and obedient is because of Bonnie Henry's soft-sell technique. Doug Ford's hard-sell tactics in Toronto have not been as effective and the protest movement there is much stronger as a result.

Bonnie Henry has just published her book of the same name. *Be Kind, Be Calm, Be Safe* is co-authored by her sister Lynn Henry who also happens to be director of publishing house Knopf Canada. The New York Times called Henry "one of the most effective public health figures in the world." She has been called "a calming voice in a sea of coronavirus madness," and "our hero" in national newspapers. Excuse me while I barf.

She is effective for several reasons. First she's a woman and generally speaking people are less threatened and intimidated by women. Women in positions of power and influence are seen as more trustworthy. Secondly, she is a medical doctor who is exhibiting compassion and concern for the general population. People are depressed, anxious and distraught and Bonnie Henry gives them all the virtual hugs and reassurance they need.

One thing we should never forget: the whole world really is in need of hugs and reassurance because we are all under attack no matter which side of the fence we are on.

We should focus most of our energy on doing all the things the Empire doesn't want us doing. The more we do these things openly and publicly, the more people will feel encouraged and strengthened by our courage and they will join us or copy our behavior elsewhere.

Stay home as little as possible. We must go out of the house. That means hanging out with each other and more importantly getting together and holding strategy meetings and conferences to discuss and finalize plans. Preferably in person and in public if possible. The more we go out into the world and go to restaurants and cafes and challenge the health orders the stronger we will become and the resistance of restaurant owners and staff will be weakened. They are not our enemies but they need to be re-taught how to be human beings and de-programmed by our presence and behavior.

We need to hug and touch each other in public displays of affectionate for the same reasons stated above. We need to make lots of music, dance and worship together and most of all publicly show joy, peace and love. Nothing can withstand these things.

We must publicly promote and take vitamins and supplements that help improve our immune systems and overall health. Things like zinc, Vitamin C and D3, hydroxychloroquine and any other safe and effective treatments that are used for influenza. The frightened masses need to be taught how to take care of their bodies and their health, and lesson their addiction and dependence on pharmaceutical medicine. Healthy people don't need Big Pharma.

And lastly, we need to protest and march and protest and march, and repeat over and over again, whenever and however possible. We cannot be content with just occasional rallies and marches. It must become our way of life. We need to be a disciplined army. Armies march. We are at war and we should never be lulled into the false sense of security that this will magically go away. We need to bring all of our resources and all of our arsenal of weapons to the table and start strategizing on how best to use them. Every city and country is different so every strategy must be tailor-made for each neighborhood and community.

CHAPTER SIX

DON'T GIVE THE ENEMY AMMUNITION

The media spin doctors are sitting on the sidelines waiting and watching for members of our movement to make mistakes so they can use these mistakes against us. Any good lawyer knows the easiest way to undermine the argument of the other side is to discredit the witnesses. Put the character of the witness on the stand instead of the substance of their testimony. Ad hominem attacks are the standard method of those without any real defense so in some ways when the enemy uses character assassinations it reveals our enemies have little defense.

The unfortunate truth is that some people within the movement make continual blunders in the media on their Facebook pages and Youtube channels. There are many of us who have large followings on Bitchute and other video sharing platforms. Some things to consider avoiding are listed here:

1. Give up on promoting politicians and political saviors. It is likely that there are few leaders in our western governments who are not bought and paid for mouthpieces of the Empire. It is extremely difficult if not impossible anymore for politicians to rise up the political ladder unless the Empire has vetted them and allowed them to continue especially not in America, the center of their operations.

2. Don't use political talking points to further the cause of the movement. A normal democracy has a left and a right wing. When one side takes over and destroys the other it's

called a dictatorship like in Soviet Russia where the left destroyed the right or in Nazi Germany where the fascists destroyed the left-wing communists. We can get back to the normal, healthy political debates about abortion, gender, immigration and other hot-button topics later. If you want to fight for freedom of speech you have to also fight for the right of those you politically oppose to have their voice heard also.

3. Don't bring topics that are out in left field into the movement. Things like UFO's, aliens and Flat Earth only give the media fuel to add to the fire. They want to brand us as lunatic fringers, conspiracy theorists and nutcases. Don't help them do that by speculating about the shape of the Earth or sharing your alien abduction story. It might be very important and urgent for you but it doesn't help us.

4. Look and dress normal. People are watching us from the streets and when they see people dressed in outrageous costumes and wearing weird hats they think we are outrageous and weird. The public desperately wants to believe we are crazy so don't help them find something to confirm their suspicions. You got to be you and for many dress is a defining statement about who they are but just consider the impact of how we present ourselves.

5. Avoid connections to political parties. Don't bring political flags promoting parties to the protests or spend time behind the microphone endorsing politicians or political parties. Do that on your own time. This isn't a conservative or a liberal movement even though there is a higher percentage of conservatives involved at the moment. We have to keep the door open for the left

wingers to get involved in our movement. Political flags and endorsements of parties or individuals doesn't help.

6. Fight for everyone's rights not just for the rights of your special interest group. We're not a Christian movement or a New Age movement so try to avoid using the movement and the microphone as an opportunity to push your religious beliefs. If you have to preach, try to speak in terms broad enough for everyone to relate to. There are many, many things spiritual people have in common so focus on those things and that will help unite us.

7. Fight for what is right and **FOR** what you believe in instead of what you oppose. Fight *for* our common issues of freedom of speech and freedom of worship instead of fighting against censorship. Fight *for* wealth equality instead of fighting against wealth inequality is another example.

8. Expose don't oppose. Shine a light on the darkness instead of trying to destroy the darkness. Educate people with facts, science and quality information about what is happening.

9. Don't attack individuals. Go after the ideas of the individuals instead, otherwise we are guilty of ad hominem attacks. Bonnie Henry is a sacred cow to Canadians and it's risky to attack the sacred cows. Be aware of her influence but avoid personal attacks.

10. Avoid racist-sounding comments and positions. Our culture isn't going to follow any movement that promotes anti-Zionism, anti-semitism, anti-Islam, anti-gay, anti-abortion, anti-BLM. You may have your own views on these subjects but they don't help us. Some people in the movement are connected to white supremacist, Neo-Nazi

groups. They don't speak for the movement, they speak for themselves.

Bring your best game to the table. We are dealing with master chess players and too often we are bringing a checkerboard to the table. Strategize your thinking. The movement needs plans and strategies. We can't win by feeding the enemy with things that make us look bad.

Don't spend all your time and energy focusing on the negative and exploring the bottomless pit of the rabbit hole. Conspiracy theory websites, articles, blogs and books focus on one aspect of our human condition and spending too much time down the rabbit hole can cause depression and even mental health issues because it's just too negative.

Balance your reading with history and science, both are more reliable than Youtube videos about Reptilians and Greys. Understanding modern history is the sure-fire way to understanding the human condition and also understanding that the Empire doesn't control everything and everyone. If they did they wouldn't be doing what they are doing right now. They want to control everything and everyone but this is a pipe dream that will never be fulfilled.

Focus more on international politics instead of American politics. Most of the MSM media is a reality TV show. It's not real. The narrative and worldview of the US media is distorted and full of propaganda about the Empire and the demonization of countries and individuals opposed to the Empire's quest for global dominance. One of the best alternative websites on the net is www.globalresearch.ca run by Canadian professor Michel Chossudovsky. There are tons of informative articles on the international scene from top writers. There are many different viewpoints expressed so it's not a political echo chamber.

Another good place to start is Wikipedia. Usually mentioning this is followed by groans of protest that Wikipedia is controlled by the Empire. That's only partially true. Wikipedia is based in San Francisco and receives millions in funding. They have a staff of almost 300 in their home office who manage the site but the bulk of the articles are created by over 80,000 volunteers from all over the world. The 1911 version of the Encyclopedia Britannica was the source of many Wikipedia articles because it's in the public domain.

All articles are cited with clickable sources. That's not saying it's the whole truth and nothing but the truth but it is a good place to start. Following the links cited can be a real eye-opener and help to give a balanced view instead of going off the deep end watching Youtube videos about Joe Biden's earlobes.

Other notable alternative outlets and there are many, many others. The list is growing rapidly as people are fleeing MSM for more reliable news:

Rebel News, Druthers, Truthdig, James Corbett

Russia Today, Dollar Vigilante, Dan Dicks

AsiaTimes, Consortium News

CHAPTER SEVEN

BUILDING BRIDGES

"We have a long way to go before we are able to hear the voices of everyone on earth, but I believe that providing voices and building bridges is essential for the World Peace we all wish for."

~ *Joichi Ito*

The protest movement that has grown over the last year is a direct reaction of the lockdown measures introduced in practically every country on Earth early in 2020. It became very obvious to those already awakened by the false flag operation of 9/11 that this pandemic was another fake media scam perpetrated by the same sociopathic elites who control the Empire.

We have focused on our human rights that are enshrined in the constitutions of our nations. The civil rights and freedoms we enjoy were paid for with the blood, sweat and tears of millions who fought in senseless wars. The Empire wants to take all these rights and freedoms away from us and we cannot allow them to do that.

These gains in civil rights were won through the American, French and Russian Revolutions combined with the two world wars and the strikes and hard negotiations of labor unions and many, many other lobby groups over the last 300 years. There are countless groups now fighting for rights for indigenous people, for equality for women, LGBTQ, Palestinians and many others. If we want to build bridges with other activists we have to support what they support. One of the big mistakes of some of the members in the movement is criticizing other activist movements like BLM instead of supporting them. Stand up for those wanting equality and leave the politics out of it. If you want to fight for freedom of speech you have to fight for freedom of speech for everyone. Some of you reading this can't or won't. Up to you.

We are all on the same team. We had Sikh farmers fighting for their rights in India joining us at the Art Gallery on several occasions. We have offered them the microphone and we have supported their cause. Other groups like the Falun Gong meet regularly at the Art Gallery. We should be making every effort to build bridges with all these groups and attempting to share our common ground of fighting for our rights and freedoms.

The local businesses are especially hurting and vulnerable to these continuing restrictions that are crushing and bankrupting them. We can make further efforts to reach out and support them and give them a voice from our weekly rallies. We have the largest regular protests in the Vancouver area and at the very least we can offer them the microphone to voice their concerns.

Others groups like the churches, temples, synagogues and mosques are still shut down and banned from holding regular services. Getting them on board with us would create powerful allies in this fight for our human rights. We can help facilitate and organize meetings with religious leaders to start a dialogue about these so-called health measures.

The other industry that has been devastated is the music industry. Most musicians have seen their careers evaporate over the last year as gigs and festivals were cancelled, night clubs, restaurants and bars were closed and severe restrictions were placed on live music. We can find liaison officers among our members who are willing to reach out to the musicians and build bridges with them instead of spending all our energies fighting over wearing masks. We have a free outdoor public stage every week where we could invite local musicians to perform. Some of them will come if invited.

We also have many, many protest groups springing up all over Canada and the rest of the world that we can keep reaching out to; the more united and connected we are, the stronger we are: united we stand, divided we fall. We don't have to agree with everything or all think the same way. We need unity not uniformity.

We need to put aside our political convictions and topics of debate. A normal, healthy democracy happens when there is public debate over issues. We can get back to the debates later but for now we need to join hands with conservatives, liberals, radicals, libertarians, anarchists, socialists, democrats and republicans. We need to open up the door and allow the Sikhs, Muslims, Jews, Catholics, Christians, New Agers, Hindus, Hare Krishnas and everyone else into our movement so we can all fight together for our freedom.

CHAPTER EIGHT

Victory is Guaranteed

We will win this war and this is guaranteed for several reasons. Before we get to that we need remind ourselves that the Empire's plans are madness and they can't possibly succeed long term. The Empire is collapsing just like all empires in history. None of them have survived. The Roman Empire slowly fell for a variety of reasons and many of them are the same reasons the current Empire is falling.

The downside is they will probably take a lot of people down with them. Every war has casualties and though difficult at the moment to estimate, the last year of the pandemic has taken its toll on the human race. At the very least we can agree they have added to the misery of the whole planet and they did nothing to increase human happiness in 2020.

The global economic system of the Empire is basically a Ponzi scheme that can only continue to exist if money is always being fed into the system. The US debt is heading towards 30 trillion dollars and the recent $1.9 trillion dollar stimulus package will push it further over that mark. It's all fake money that is printed out of thin air. It provides temporary relief to the Empire's financial holdings but creates more inflation and drives the poor and working class into more poverty.

Here is a brief list of all the reasons why the Empire will fail and why we will defeat them:

1. Good always triumphs over evil. The universe is not a blind automaton without purpose or meaning. The universe is built on the principles of love: it is a *good* universe. That doesn't mean the universe will suddenly wave a magic wand and all our problems will disappear. It also doesn't mean that it will be easy to overcome the Empire. The real issue for us is not *if we will win* but *when* and *how* we will win and the how is the most important thing to consider. The way we fight this battle is also the way forward to building a new and better world.

2. The plans of the elites are a House of Cards. Their plans are like a plot from a Marvel Comic Book where deranged madmen try to take over the world with diabolical vaccines and artificial intelligence. No wonder people don't believe us when we try to tell them what the Empire has in store for the world. It sounds crazy because it is crazy. Only time will prove us right. Many people might have to suffer first before things get bad enough for people to wake up.

3. There will be a popular revolt. History has shown that sooner or later the working classes will rise up by the thousands and millions and overthrow tyranny. It has usually been through the mismanagement and greed of overlords that resulted in famine and unemployment for the average person. Their anger will build like a pot of boiling water until eventually it will boil over and the people will rise up in a spontaneous revolt. We don't know when or what spark will ignite the fire but it isn't our job to light the fire. It is our job to cut the wood and build the fire and wait for the spark to come. It will come if we work hard and if we are patient.

4. The human soul is eternal. We mentioned earlier that this is a full frontal assault on the human soul. The Empire sincerely wants to rid the world of our inner soul. They despise humanity because, in their arrogance they believe themselves to be a separate race, a master race of superhuman gods. The human soul cannot be destroyed however because it is made out of an eternal substance we usually call *spirit*.

5. The sun is going down. When the sun is going down on the horizon it looks the same as if it is coming up. The Empire sociopaths have made the mistake in believing that the sun is coming up but the truth is their Empire is collapsing. The New World Order is not new either. It is just the same old world system of profit, greed and power that has served them well but is in its death throes. There are millions of people who don't want their world anymore.

6. Their economic system is unsustainable. The derivatives market and Wall Street stock market economy is a giant Ponzi scheme that will eventually collapse under its own weight. It's just a matter of time. The international fractional reserve banking system created by the Empire is bankrupt. The oil industry which is the other half of the Empire's power and wealth is also going down: the easy oil is all gone long ago and that's why they have to get oil out of the tar sands in Alberta. The banking and oil Empire is in its final days.

7. Their plans involve far too many players. It is not possible for them with their empty soulless ideology to consolidate and coordinate all the countries, media, technology, companies, corporations and economies.

Human beings are bonded together through the family, the community and then their societies and nations. Family is the basic unit of society and the Empire's plans to destroy families will also destroy their plans. It's like someone trying to fix a boat by drilling holes in the hull.

8. They will make more and more mistakes. Because the world system they want to create is so complicated and complex they will begin to make more and more mistakes as they try to put it together. Like a machine that is too complex, it will fall apart once it is started up. Their lies will compound themselves and it will become more and more obvious to people they are lying.

9. Criminals always have infighting. The Empire is a criminal organization that is involved in all areas of corrupt criminal activity like drugs, sex trafficking, prostitution, gambling and pornography. It is guaranteed they fight and tear each other apart like wolves. As their empire begins to unravel and all their plans start to fall apart they will turn on each other and start killing each other off. The paranoid top bosses will engage in assassinations of those they consider threats or rivals. Hitler purged a thousand of his own Nazi leaders in the *Night of the Long Knives* from June 30 to July 2, 1934. Purges create fear but they also create enemies and resentment that comes back to haunt the perpetrators. Hitler had several attempts on his life by his own men.

10. Mutinies will come. The Empire has millions of agents and flunkies all over the world. Many have done the bidding of the elites because they have profited from the system and it has benefited them financially. But these are opportunistic, selfish men and women and they will turn tail and run if things don't go their way. Selfish people are only loyal to money and power and if there is nothing in it for them, they will bail out. Other members got into it because they were recruited at a young age and were naive and gullible enough to believe the Empire was doing good things for the world. As they moved up the ladder they become disillusioned with the Empire once they realize what kind of people they are and what they really want.

In conclusion, we must have faith and be confident that good will eventually win and defeat the Evil Empire. Faith is the number one requirement to fight this battle for the soul of planet Earth.

There are two primary forces in this world, fear and faith. Fear can move you to destructiveness or sickness or failure. Only in rare instances will it motivate you to accomplishment. But faith is a greater force. Faith can drive itself into your consciousness and set you free from fear forever.

~ Norman Vincent Peale

CHAPTER NINE

CELL GROUPS

Various organizations have used cell groups successfully to build their membership, provide structure and de-centralize their organization. Most importantly cell groups allow organizations to get everyone involved if only to socialize. Protestant Christian churches have long used this method to strengthen their communities. Many churches call them "care groups" and there is emphasis on giving each other moral support, reading the Bible together and praying for each other.

Other less benevolent organizations have used cells to promote military agendas. Small autonomous cell groups of anywhere from 3 to a dozen members were effectively employed by the French underground resistance in WW2 and by the IRA (Irish Republican Army). These groups used cell groups to prevent infiltration. A large top-down organization with a centralized command is easy to infiltrate because nefarious outside counter-intelligence groups only need to send in one agent. A proliferation of independent cells who have their own agendas, plans and leadership is much harder to infiltrate because many undercover agents are needed and small groups have trusted members who are known to everyone in the group and resist outsiders coming in.

Each cell group can have its own plans and activities. There doesn't need to be, nor is it desirable at this crucial time in world history for there to be a handful of leaders doing all the work while the majority of activists remain idle waiting for someone to show them them what to do. All hands on deck. We all need to get involved and do something.

The word *activist* is based on the word *act*. An activist does something. We all have different skills, abilities, temperaments and strengths. Cell groups allow like-minded and socially compatible activists to organize themselves and find a project or plan they can accomplish together.

At the very least, cell groups can help give each other moral support and help us rebuild our communities in more positive directions. It's better than staying at home, isolated and depressed, drinking too much alcohol and worrying about the future. Ten heads are better than one and teamwork is needed more than ever.

Recruiting

Though it is true we are still relatively small in number, the overall movement can grow significantly when we are all established into cells groups. Then we can start recruiting new people. It is much easier for people to join a small cell group than to join a big rally where there are way too many people and confusion. The real secret of successful activism is careful planning by small teams who come up with a campaign and carry it out.

Never underestimate the power of a small motivated group of people. The rallies give people the illusion that the speakers are doing everything and they are the sole leaders in the movement but the reality is that there are many people working behind the scenes. Decide today to be on of those people and start your own cell group. Be a leader.

CHAPTER TEN

PUBLIC MARKET

T housands of small businesses closed down in 2020 and many of them closed permanently. Any drive-by of retail neighborhoods in Vancouver will reveal hundreds of For Lease signs up over empty storefronts. The devastation to the local economies all over Canada, the USA and the rest of the world has been unprecedented. Almost 100,000 businesses in the US closed down as of September 2020 and that number is surely climbing.

Small and medium businesses represent over 90% of the business force and 70% were closed in 2020. About 30% of those are closed permanently. Meanwhile the mega-billionaires are busy buying up and monopolizing whole industries. Bill Gates, the ubiquitous virus-peddler is now owner of 245,000 acres of land in the USA and Elon Musk and Jeff Bezos' wealth has skyrocketed.

The very rapidly approaching Vaccine Passports are a signal to all of us what the Empire has in store for the vaccinated and the unvaccinated. Our ability to work, live, shop and go to restaurants and clubs will be determined by our willingness to submit to an untested, experimental vaccine.

All of this means our ability to make a living will be limited in the coming years. These changes, if the Empire is successful will be permanent. Those of us who are not willing to comply with the sociopaths' demands will need to find other means to create wealth and trade.

We will be forced to create our own economies. This means taking a step back from our local economies and becoming more independent and more connected to our own community of like-minded people. We will need a common public market. This means we will have to return to a simple system of barter and exchange of goods or come up with a common currency to trade.

The weekly rallies are the ideal place to start a public market. We are all there anyway and the beginning of this is already underway as people are setting up tables to sell T-shirts and hats and snacks to raise money to fund their small organizations. If you made a donation to buy this book thank you! You are helping to build our new economy!

There isn't a lot of time to waste. The biggest problem for all of us may very well be food. We should be looking at renting warehouse space and stockpiling food. If this isn't feasible yet then we should at least begin stocking up on food items like rice, canned food and other non-perishables. We need enough food for each of us and our families to get through the winter. Remember the Boy Scout motto: Be Prepared!

CHAPTER ELEVEN

THE MARCHES

"He who passively accepts evil is as much involved in it as he who helps to perpetrate it. He who accepts evil without protesting against it is really cooperating with it."

~ Martin Luther King, Jr.

The following are some marches and protests with relatively small numbers that were very effective and brought lasting change. Generally large numbers are helpful but many protests and marches with very high numbers have resulted in no change to the government policies they protested against while small protests had enormous results. Terry Fox's run across Canada was really a protest of one and he single-handedly raised millions for cancer research.

Denmark Pots and Pans

In November of 2020, the Danish government introduced legislation that would force people infected with Covid-19 to take mandatory medical examinations, hospitalized and placed in isolation. The government wanted to force certain groups of people to be vaccinated and those who refused could be detained. Thousands of Danish people took to the streets armed with pots and pans and protested for nine days straight until the government backed down and rescinded these laws.

This is encouraging because it shows that governments can be forced to step back through the power of peaceful but prolonged protest. It also showed that a different approach is needed: banging pots and pans relentlessly had a psychological affect on the government leaders. The relentless, repetitive and loud noise frightened the politicians and they realized or imagined it was a threat to their existence. History has shown that ***politicians are afraid of the people*** and the power of the people is still stronger than the most powerful institutions.

The Salt March

The British East India Company had established a tax on salt in India in the late 1800's in order to make British salt competitive with the higher grade Indian salt. The tax made salt unaffordable for most of India's majority poor population. Salt is a necessity in Indian diet due to the loss of salt from perspiration in India's very hot, dry climate.

In 1930 Mahatma Gandhi organized a march from Ahmedabad to Dandi on the coast, a 24-day journey of 240 miles to protest this unfair tax which resulted in the deaths of countless Indians due to iodine deficiency and leprosy induced by lack of salt. The Salt March started with just Gandhi and 78 of his followers but grew to thousands who joined along the way. Gandhi, along with 60,000 others were arrested and jailed for their actions which resulted in world-wide attention on the plight of India at the hands of the British.

The Salt March also sparked widespread civil disobedience in India as millions began collecting and making salt in defiance of British law. It also touched off a wave of boycotts of British goods and numerous other refusals to pay other taxes. The British implemented tougher laws and restrictions on the newly-founded Indian Congress but to no avail: the people were energized.

The British were confused and shaken by the non-violent protests; many confessed they would prefer violence as they had no established policies on how to deal with these types of protests. One British officer later wrote he felt nauseous whenever he had to deal with the Indian Congress; Winston Churchill saw the actions of Gandhi whom he called a "half-naked fakir" as the beginning of the end of the British Empire and Jawaharlal Nehru, the first Prime Minister of India later remarked:

"Of course these movements exercised tremendous pressure on the British Government and shook the government machinery. But the real importance, to my mind, lay in the effect they had on our own people, and especially the village masses...Non-cooperation dragged them out of the mire and gave them self-respect and self-reliance..."

Boston Tea Party

The Boston Tea Party, Dec.16, 1773, was the first significant act of rebellion by American colonists against the British. For years, colonists were unfairly taxed by the British government without representation in Parliament, and the Tea Act of 1773, which granted a monopoly and tax exemption to the British East Indian Company, was the final straw that caused American opposition.

Sixty men led by the Sons of Liberty disguised themselves as Native Americans on Dec. 16, 1773, and threw 342 chests – 92,000 pounds – of tea into the Boston Harbor. The protest was met with punishment from the British as Parliament passed punitive measures, such as closing Boston's port until the debt from the Boston Tea Party was paid, and housing British troops in American homes, through the Intolerable Acts that aimed to target Massachusetts and divide the other colonies. Instead, it sparked the First Continental Congress in 1774 and led to the American Revolution, which began in Massachusetts in 1775 and ended in 1783 when the British formally recognized U.S. independence.

The Monday Demonstrations, 1982-1989

What started as a weekly prayer meeting turned into a movement that helped bring down the Berlin Wall. In 1982, a German pastor started a weekly prayer service on Mondays to spread the message of peace in the middle of the ongoing Cold War. Soon, people from all ages and religious backgrounds began seeking weekly sanctuary in his church. A dozen people grew to thousands of people, despite German officials' efforts to blockade the streets around the church. Right before the wall came down, around 300,000 peaceful protestors gathered on a Monday in late October of 1989. One week later, the Berlin Wall was knocked down, reuniting West and East Germany.

The Protestant Reformation

The Protestant Reformation is a poignant reminder that sometimes all it takes is one spark to start a fire. Martin Luther is widely credited for being the spark that started the Protestant Reformation, a movement that completely upended the Catholic Church and changed the way that people practiced religion on a global scale. One man's voice, in the form of the list of *95 Theses* that he nailed to the door of the Wittenberg Church in 1517 was enough to create an entirely new religious sect (that literally has the word "protest" in its name).

Theatre, Music, Worship, Dance, Comedy

If you have decided to follow with this indirect strategy instead of a confrontational one, then another method is by using the rallies and marches as an opportunity for theatre, music, worship, dance and comedy as weapons in our arsenal. Remember the Empire wants to rid us of our traditional culture so they can introduce their crackpot culture.

Whatever they don't want, we have to give it them, in spades. Comedy is especially effective against political tyranny and in medieval times, it was used extensively to ridicule and poke fun of the monarchy. Traveling bards and circus shows went from town to town and held impromptu outdoor entertainment wherever they went. Something like this could even be revived as our government and so-called health ministers have cancelled culture indefinitely. It is their plan to never bring it back.

In the meantime, it would be beneficial and relatively easy to unleash the talents of so many of us who are actors, musicians, artists, comedians and spiritual worshipers. The rallies are perfect opportunities because we have ourselves as a live audience. We can pass the hat for the entertainers to help support them and also create entertainment that will appeal to those passersby who might not listen to a speech but would be open to something that doesn't cause friction in their programmed mind. The idea is to create an opportunity for people to experience that eureka moment, that ah-ha emotional reaction when they realize they've been programmed, brainwashed and lied to.

Live worship services and spiritual connection is very important and we should encourage people of all faiths to bring their services, rituals, worship, celebrations and festivals to the rallies. The Empire doesn't want us to have any spirituality anymore. They want a barren, soulless religion of atheism that has symbols but no meaning, rituals but no values; and secular priests who believe in nothing. Their idea of utopia is the Planet Vulcan where cold, indifferent Spock leaders rule over us, devoid of emotion and empathy.

CHAPTER TWELVE

MEDIA WARFARE

Freedom of speech is under attack on Youtube, Twitter and Facebook. Thousands of people in the last year had their accounts deleted on all platforms without warning and without appeal. How do we fight these tech giants who have no oversight from government?

Thousands, even millions have fled Twitter, Youtube and Facebook to join other platforms like Bitchute, Parler, Rumble and BrandNewTube. More platforms are on the way. This is a good thing if we want to protect our right to speak freely in the public arena. The downside is that these groups can become giant echo chambers where there is only one voice heard. Democracy means we have a public debate about any subject that is relevant to the nation or society.

How do we engage in a campaign of education and deprogramming of our poor lost brothers and sisters who have been thoroughly brainwashed by these same tech giants and mainstream media?

One thing that is more effective than other methods on social media is using memes, especially funny ones. A short, sharp message that pokes fun of an idea is much more effective than a 30-page article or asking a friend to watch a 2-hour video about PCR tests. Most people have no time or patience. Humor cuts through the brainwashing.

Short videos and articles are better than long ones. A 2-minute video that sums up the idea is often far better. We are only trying to plant seeds and stir up an interest in our side of the story. We want to try and turn the wheels in their brain to start thinking in a different direction. As we mentioned earlier, the most important thing is to first convince them the media is lying and brainwashing people. This isn't that hard because most people already have a low opinion of journalists and the media.

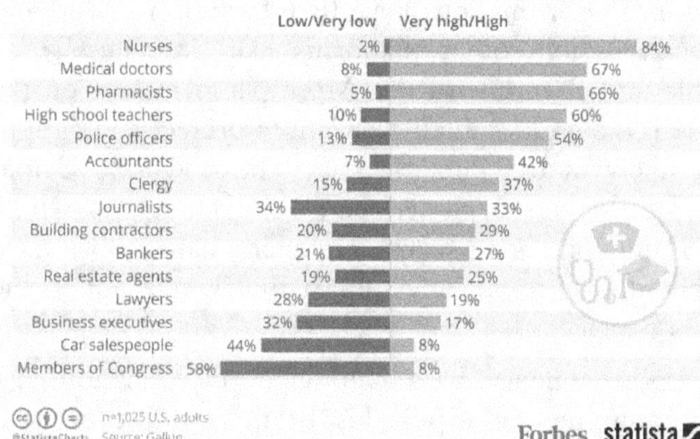

A recent survey ranked nurses as the number one most trusted profession. This has been the same ranking for 19 years now so we are also dealing with a population that has put enormous faith in nurses and doctors. We can use this to our advantage by allowing and encouraging nurses and doctors to speak publicly at the rallies. That means we have to reach out to them and get them to overcome their fear of losing their jobs. Not an easy thing for them. Nobody wants to have their career ruined.

If you are already active on social media, then you know how easy it is to lose people. One wrong comment or if you share fake news, people will stop following you. Credibility is very important. There is tons of disinfo out there, much of it is created by the agents of the Empire to cause confusion, distraction and division so try really hard to share only the best articles and videos.

Slacktivism

Genuine social media activism is supported by concrete actions, donations, and measurable commitments to change. Without offline action, gestures like using a hashtag or posting videos come across as performative, opportunistic, and lazy. Critics are often quick to call out these minimal efforts as "slacktivism."

We need boots on the ground. We can't win a war solely on the internet. People who only come out to the big rallies and demand time to give long speeches about their organizations would be more effective if they came to all the marches. Stop posting, start marching.

The aim of social activism is to disrupt the status quo. We're not here to grease the machinery, we are here to pour sand into the Empire's plans and jam their agenda until the machine breaks down and quits. Then we will bring in our machine to replace it. If we want to go on an offensive campaign on social media, the people to go after are the people promoting these draconian measures like our health ministers, premiers, MSM outlets and politicians. Most of the comments on the posts of our government leaders are an uncoordinated effort. Small teams of social media warriors would be far more effective and damaging to their flimsy lies.

Arguing and fighting with brainwashed people often works against us because we appear belligerent, aggressive and hostile. The brainwashed people aren't our enemy. Our enemy is the Empire and its bought-and-paid-for stooges and agents who are bribed with millions of dollars tucked away in offshore accounts.

These men and women are traitors. They are guilty of the highest crime in society – treason against their own people. Leaders in positions of trust who have willfully betrayed that trust and openly lied and manipulated the people for personal gain will be put on trial and judged. That's where this is all heading: Nuremberg 2.0 is coming.

Appeal to the Left

Vancouver is a left-leaning city in Canada. The interior of BC is much more conservative according to voting records. Canadians in general are not as gun-happy or religiously conservative as Americans and Vancouverites are no exception. One thing Canadians value is inclusivity. We are a multi-cultural, multi-ethnic country. Vancouver is 46% Asian population and only 40% European descent.

For whatever reasons, conservatives so far are more clued in to what is going on than liberals. We can keep preaching to the choir but if we want to wake up the liberal sheep we have to tailor our message to appeal to them. Same thing can be said for minority groups like Sikhs, Chinese, Taiwanese and East Indians. Millenials today are much more liberal-leaning and brainwashed than the boomers. They are also the most tolerant and inclusive generation in history. Any attacks by rally people on gender issues or BLM will only drive them away. Most of them are huddled on Tik Tok, Snapchat and Instagram as well as gaming sites like Discord and Twitch. We need to attract and recruit young people who are on these social media sites already to help get the millenials to wake up.

A recent study of Vancouver found that:

- Metro Vancouver can be a hard place to make friends.

- Our neighborhood connections are cordial, but weak.

- We prefer to keep to ourselves, or have little interest in getting to know our neighbors.

- Many people in metro Vancouver are retreating from community life.

This may help answer why Vancouver has such low numbers at the rallies and why Vancouver has submitted so readily to the lockdown measures compared to Montreal or Toronto. Vancouverites were already isolated and staying at home so the lockdown measures didn't bother them as much.

CHAPTER THIRTEEN

HEALTH iS A WEAPON

We are in the beginning of a medical war perpetrated by the WHO, Big Pharma and its agents Bill Gates and Tony Fauci. They are working in coordination with national and local health ministers and medical professionals to advance their "final solution" (Bill Gates' actual words). They have weaponized the healthcare industry and are using it along with the media in a fake kindness and fake compassion campaign. Bonne Henry's fake slogan *Be Kind, Be Safe, Be Calm* has been one of their most effective tools.

Vaccines have been promoted from the beginning of this fake pandemic as the *only solution* to stop Covid-19. However, those of us who are educated and informed by the natural health professionals and naturopaths know that there are a variety of ways to treat influenza or any disease for that matter. We have a plethora of tools in our war chest to use to build up the immune system and to fight any disease.

"The doctor of the future will give no medicine but will interest his patients in the care of the human frame, in diet and in the cause and prevention of disease."

~ Thomas Edison

There is a war going on for decades between the pharmaceutical industry and the natural health industry. There is no money to be made in a healthy population. Only sick people can be fed drugs and only sick people can make money for the drug dealers of Big Pharma.

The goal of all health care ought to be to make people happy because happy people are rarely sick and sick people are rarely happy. Holistic medicine is concerned with the whole person, his or her physical, emotional, spiritual and mental health. Pharmaceutical medicine is preoccupied with fighting battles against our bodies and often the damage done by the pharmaceutical medicine is equal to or greater than the cure.

There are thousands of well-documented cases of vaccine injured and murdered people who took vaccines because they trusted the medical industry and they trusted their healthcare providers.

A failure of reason has descended over mass society and the idea has become ingrained in people's minds that vaccines are the only tool available for the Covid-19 health crisis. Influenza and upper respiratory diseases have been treated with a variety of methods for centuries and this has not changed. Health professionals all over the world are using many different means of treating this virus:

Molnupiravir

A new experimental drug is being tested and shows promise of eliminating COVID-19 just by taking a pill. The pill, Molnupiravir, which is being developed by Ridgeback Biotherapeutics and Merck (MRK), was found to reduce the virus in individuals after five days of treatment in a mid-stage study, the companies announced in a release on March 6.

While more studies of Molnupiravir are underway, the companies say the pill could provide a viable way to treat those that have symptoms of COVID-19 and be the first oral antiviral drug to combat the virus.

Dr. Marc Siegel in an interview stated that the pill "may be the holy grail on this because it was just studied in phase two trials and it literally stopped the virus in its tracks. And there wasn't any virus found in the patients that were studied."

Arbidol

Doctors in Wuhan have aggressively treated patients with antivirals not approved in the U.S. The drug they utilized most often was Arbidol, manufactured by the Russian company JSC Pharmstandard. One preliminary study showed that Arbidol could drastically improve chest CT scans and speed the body's clearing of the virus, perhaps by inhibiting viral replication.

Traditional Chinese Medicine

"It is a legal health system in China which is parallel with Western medicine, and of course, there is also integration between traditional medicine and Western medicine," Dr. Jianping Liu, professor of clinical epidemiology at the Beijing University of Chinese Medicine, told NBC News.

"It's a holistic approach."

The main herbal formulas recommended for treatment of COVID-19 are jinhua qinggan capsules, lianhua qingwen capsules and shufeng jiedu capsules, according to Liu. These remedies consist of a combination of dozens of herbs, Liu said.

Hydroxychloroquine

This medicine has been FDA approved for 65 years, given to pregnant women, breastfeeding women, children, the elderly and the immune-compromised for decades without complication. An ongoing media campaign against it has been waged to stop its use by the general public. It is blatantly obvious that the vaccine companies don't have any interest in people's health.

HCQ Explained: excellent video presentation of how it works:

www.americasfrontlinedoctors.com/references/science-of-hcq/

Favipiravir

The antiviral drug Favipiravir, approved in Japan and China, according to a sizable randomized clinical trial could be more effective than Arbidol. Additional research is needed but these early studies are promising. Given COVID-19's swift expansion, there should be plenty of opportunities to explore their potential.

Interferon Alfa 2b

Cuba also offers treatment regimens, some of which are not available in the United States. A key component of the protocols being used on the island and in the medical missions is Cuba's Interferon Alfa 2B Recombinant (IFNrec). Scientific journals like the Lancet and the World Journal of Pediatrics have recognized the impact of IFNrec. It has been used against various viral infections for which there are no specific therapies available, having demonstrated its ability to activate the patient's immune system and to inhibit viral replication.

Natural Health Treatments:

- Lauricidin, a monoloaurin supplement. Take between meals. Coats the biofilms of viruses, yeast and bad bacteria.
- Alkaline Colloidal Silver Water. A natural alternative to antibiotics.
- Liposomal Vitamin C for enhanced absorption without upsetting the gastrointestinal system.
- Pure zinc liquid drops to restore the sense of taste and smell and boost the immune system.
- 20 ounces of juices or smoothies daily.
- Immunomax powder to boost your immune system.
- High quality vitamin D.
- Biodetox to reduce pain and inflammation.
- Dairy free probiotic.
- Turmeric, pepper and honey tea to reduce inflammation and pain and boost your immune system.

More info:

www.catherinecarrigan.com/natural-healing-remedies-for-covid-19/

CHAPTER FOURTEEN

SIX PRINCIPLES OF NON-VIOLENCE

by Dr. Martin Luther King Jr.

As a theologian, Martin Luther King wrote about his "pilgrimage to nonviolence" in his first book, *Stride Toward Freedom*. In subsequent books and articles he reflected often on his understanding of nonviolence. "True pacifism or nonviolent resistance," King wrote, is "a courageous confrontation of evil by the power of love." Committed to nonviolence, King believed that "the Christian doctrine of love operating through the Gandhian method of nonviolence was one of the most potent weapons available to oppressed people in their struggle for freedom." The following are his Six Principles of Non-Violence:

PRINCIPLE ONE: Nonviolence is a way of life for courageous people.

• It is active nonviolent resistance to evil.

• It is aggressive spiritually, mentally and emotionally.

PRINCIPLE TWO: Nonviolence seeks to win friendship and understanding.

• The end result of nonviolence is redemption and reconciliation.

• The purpose of nonviolence is the creation of the Beloved Community.

PRINCIPLE THREE: Nonviolence seeks to defeat injustice not people.

•Nonviolence recognizes that evildoers are also victims and are not evil people.

•The nonviolent resister seeks to defeat evil not people.

PRINCIPLE FOUR: Nonviolence holds that suffering can educate and transform.

•Nonviolence accepts suffering without retaliation.

•Unearned suffering is redemptive and has tremendous educational and transforming possibilities.

PRINCIPLE FIVE: Nonviolence chooses love instead of hate.

•Nonviolence resists violence of the spirit as well as the body.

•Nonviolent love is spontaneous, unmotivated, unselfish and creative.

PRINCIPLE SIX: Nonviolence believes that the universe is on the side of justice.

•The nonviolent resister has deep faith that justice will eventually win.

Nonviolence believes that God is a God of justice.

***

In addition to the six principles, Dr. King developed a six-step process to help people bring about social change in a nonviolent way.

Step 1: Gather Information

Learn all you can about the problems you see in your community through the media, social and civic organizations, and by talking to the people involved.

Step 2: Educate Others

Armed with your new knowledge, it is your duty to help those around you, such as your neighbors, relatives, friends and co-workers, better understand the problems facing society. Build a team of people devoted to finding solutions. Be sure to include those who will be directly affected by your work.

Step 3: Remain Committed

Accept that you will face many obstacles and challenges as you and your team try to change society. Agree to encourage and inspire one another along the journey.

Step 4: Peacefully Negotiate

Talk with both sides. go to the people in your community who are in trouble and who are deeply hurt by society's ills. Also go to those people who are contributing to the breakdown of a peaceful society. Use humor, intelligence and grace to lead to solutions that benefit the greater good.

Step 5: Take Action Peacefully

This step is often used when negotiation fails to produce results, or when people need to draw broader attention to a problem. it can include tactics such as peaceful demonstrations, letter-writing and petition campaign.

Step 6: Reconcile

Keep all actions and negotiations peaceful and constructive. Agree to disagree with some people and with some groups as you work to improve society. Show all involved the benefits of changing, not what they will give up by changing.

CHAPTER FIFTEEN

RADIO SILENCE

The Empire has implemented its plans, policies and agendas over the decades through covert, subversive means. They have maintained a Fabian Strategy as we have discussed previously. We propose to use this strategy against the Empire in order to reverse engineer their social engineering, psychological operations and media propaganda.

The French underground during WW2 operated resistance cells that engaged in guerrilla warfare activities, were also publishers of underground newspapers, providers of first-hand intelligence information, and maintainers of escape networks that helped Allied soldiers and airmen trapped behind enemy lines. They did this all covertly.

Is it wise to broadcast all our activities all over the internet, posting endless videos and zoom conferences? Or are we better off going underground and disappearing from sight, covering our tracks and remaining as invisible as possible? For those in the movement who are public social media warriors, the thought of shutting down their accounts and staying off the internet is probably a horrifying idea.

Millions of people have already been censored and driven off Facebook, Twitter and Youtube. Some of the new platforms that are springing up are managed by agents of the Empire. Parler, for example is owned by Robert Mercer's daughter Rebekah Mercer. Robert Mercer is heavily involved with Artificial Intelligence and he was the cash cow behind data-mining company Cambridge Analytica.

We are dealing with an invisible enemy of men who rarely reveal themselves in public. During times of war, enemy combatants engage in covert operations to conceal the source of the attack. This creates plausible deniability. This is exactly what the agents of the Empire have been doing with this biological weapon attack in the last year. A virus is impossible to track and it can never be connected to the elites.

An order for *Radio Silence* is generally issued by the military where any radio transmission may reveal troop positions, either audibly from the sound of talking, or by radio direction finding. The Freedom Movement could use this method to great effect by ceasing public broadcasting on social media of our plans, activities and agendas. This will also prevent the MSM from using all our media against us. You can't target an enemy you can't see.

CHAPTER SIXTEEN

CAMPAIGN, CAMPAIGN, CAMPAIGN

Excerpts from *How We Win* by George Lakey:

DIRECT ACTION CAMPAIGNS

Women gained the right to vote in Britain and the United States through direct action campaigns. Greenpeace used direct action to arouse the world to pass a ban on commercial whaling. Independence-minded people in Ghana and Hungary campaigned and overthrew imperial rule. Students in the United States and Britain pushed their colleges and universities into divesting holdings in fossil fuel companies. Puerto Ricans forced the U.S. Navy to stop using their islands for target practice.

Direct action is hardly a new technique. The GNAD, a searchable online database of campaigns developed at Swarthmore College, shows that successful campaigns have been waged for millennia, by workers, farmers, neighborhoods, indigenous peoples, and many other kinds of groups. Mass nonviolent direct action campaigns have even overthrown dictators in many countries—including tyrants backed by military power.

As a concept, however, such campaigns remain outside mainstream political discourse. A nonviolent direct action campaign typically makes a demand for one or more specific changes, identifies an opponent or "target" that can respond, and generates a series of nonviolent tactics that escalate over time.

Considering the drama often accompanying the campaigners' actions, it's curious that the concept of a "nonviolent campaign" remains little known. When people talk about how to mobilize power, direct action campaigning is usually ignored. Some will think of volunteering for someone running for office—a different kind of campaign. Most people find that the options that occur to them are lobbying, letter-writing, circulating petitions, or going to a protest.

A DIRECT ACTION CAMPAIGN IS NOT A PROTEST

Protests are well known, and popular. The trouble is, when I look back on the one-off protests I've joined over the years, I don't remember a single one that changed the policy we were protesting. In February 2003 I joined millions of others around the world on the eve of George W. Bush's invasion of Iraq. The protest did get a huge front-page headline in The New York Times, but Bush needed only to wait until we went home.

The New York Times said the global anti-war protest indicated a "second global superpower," but the Times overestimated. A one-off protest is for venting, not for exerting power. On that day I realized that the protest would not prevent Bush's war, because the protest's leadership didn't tell us what we could do next, and how we would escalate after that—how we would take the offensive. The leadership didn't offer us a campaign.

Bush had a plan to persist. We did not. Even today, the peace movement has not recovered from this false start, despite the American majority's fairly consistent opposition to the war. Because of the poor strategic choice to mount a one-off protest, discouragement and inaction followed. In order to build the kind of power that creates change, we needed a direct action campaign that harnessed a series of actions into an escalating sequence. The typical protest is organizationally hollow, unsustainable, and not really a problem for a strong opponent, which above all fears our staying power.

The campaigns of the civil rights movement, for the most part, had that staying power. Open violence was widely used to resist the demand for justice; local and state law enforcement joined the racist resistance. The federal government usually refused to back up the movement, or even to protect the participants.

Despite those odds, a decade of campaigns achieved major changes. Each civil rights campaign had its "target": a department store or restaurant or school board or bus company. As the community organization teachers at the Midwest Academy point out, a target is an entity able to say "yes" to the campaign's demand. When a campaign inspires other campaigns, the sum of them becomes a movement. Today we see the same phenomenon: a cluster of campaigns related to a theme becomes a movement, like the struggle for a living wage or the fight against oil and gas pipelines.

Campaigns are very different from protests because they are built for sustainability and escalation. The four brave Greensboro, North Carolina, students who ignited the civil rights sit-in movement on February 1, 1960, did not plan a oneoff protest; they understood that they could not desegregate the lunch counter without returning again and again, no matter how often they were arrested or beaten up. What's more, these were black students who knew full well that black people take extra risk when they do civil disobedience.

One reason why observers wonder if the Black Lives Matter activists have staying power is because it is unclear how many of the local protests against killings by police are transforming into genuine campaigns with winnable demands, targets that can yield those demands, and a strategy for growth and escalation. After all, without that transformation, there is no reason to expect an increase in justice, despite the heartbreak of continued killings of unarmed black people. Systemic abusive police practices, rooted in a culture of impunity, are impervious to expressions of outrage; it takes sustained power to force a real shift.

Protests are usually organized to express grief, anger, or plain opposition to an action or policy. If the event is well attended, a protest may be repeated. Campaigners, by contrast, plan from the start to do a series of nonviolent actions and continue until the goal is reached.

Campaigns give us feedback on how we're doing, so we can refine our tactics. The impact of one-off protests is tough to measure, making it hard to see how we can improve. Campaigns, more than protests, benefit from training, and training develops participants for the long run. Training incorporates new participants and meets specific needs, like better communication across barriers of race, class, and gender.

Training promotes a robust learning curve, essential for the campaign to win and also for grooming future leaders. True, winning may take weeks, or months, or years.

British students maintained a boycott of Barclays Bank that took 18 years to force the bank to divest from apartheid South Africa. Most campaigns secure their victories in a much shorter time. America's earliest recorded nonviolent campaign after European settlement was in colonial Jamestown, Virginia, when Polish artisans —the first non-English settlers—campaigned for the right to vote equally with the English. The Poles won their demand in three months.

I know of no country that has undergone major change through one-off protests. Opponents realize that no matter how many people participate in sporadic protests, participants will go home again. Winning major demands requires staying power and, as this guide will share, much else besides.

A CAMPAIGN HAS SPECIFIC DEMANDS AND A TARGET

Nonviolent campaigners know what they want: clean water in North Dakota for the Dakota Sioux people, the Dream Act for students brought to this country as children by undocumented immigrants, a cleanup of chemicals for the neighborhood of Love Canal, university paraphernalia made by workers who are treated fairly with safe working conditions. When indigenous tribes in California occupied Ward Valley as part of their campaign to preserve sacred land, they prevented the establishment of a nuclear waste dump.

Campaigners also know who can make the decision they need. Alice Paul led the National Woman's Party direct action campaign for suffrage and targeted President Woodrow Wilson. As the film Iron Jawed Angels reveals, the women in their demonstrations during World War I compared the president to the German emperor, calling him "Kaiser Wilson"! When, many years later, I interviewed Alice Paul, she said she remembered being confident that President Wilson could make the difference in persuading a balky Congress to pass the 19th Amendment so women could vote. She was right. Her group picketed the White House—at that time unheard of —and once arrested, went on hunger strikes. Her 1917 escalation of the campaign brought the vote to women in just three years.

THE ART OF ESCALATION

The 1960s civil rights movement became expert in locating and sequencing its actions for a campaign in such a way as to increase the pressure on their target. When President John F. Kennedy refused Martin Luther King Jr.'s request for support for a civil rights bill, the Southern Christian Leadership Conference (SCLC) made an unusual strategic decision. Instead of doing what was customary, which was to focus action in the nation's capital in order to gain a victory there, the SCLC decided to escalate in Birmingham, Alabama, at that time a major industrial city. The Reverend Fred Shuttlesworth, a member of SCLC, had for years led an ongoing campaign in Birmingham for equal accommodations.

In spring 1963, SCLC brought additional organizers and trainers to town, along with the charisma of Martin Luther King Jr., to join the local struggle. The campaigners escalated their tactics, confronting the segregationists' police dogs and fire hoses with nonviolent discipline. The federal government was drawn in by the level of dislocation of the city. As numbers in the campaign grew it became possible to "invade" the downtown business area, creating a crisis and forcing business owners to negotiate. An agreement was finally reached, which held despite the violence from spoilers who hoped to maintain tight racial segregation.

CAMPAIGN + CAMPAIGN + CAMPAIGN = MOVEMENT

The 1963 success in Birmingham elevated the civil rights movement to a national level. That sequence began in 1955 with the Montgomery bus boycott, significant for Alabama but not yet for the South. In town after southern town, small campaigns were waged in the following years with modest successes.

After the four college students initiated their sit-in campaign in Greensboro, students in other locations quickly followed suit. Within a month there were student sit-ins around the South and a small solidarity campaign at Woolworth stores in northern cities as well. In 1961 the Congress of Racial Equality (CORE) launched a different campaign, the Freedom Rides, to integrate interstate buses. By 1963's Birmingham campaign, participants were calling it "the Freedom Movement," and it grew very rapidly from there.

This is only one of many examples of how multiple campaigns create a movement with power that no one campaign could develop.

*to download free copy of *How We Win*:

https://archive.org/details/
GeorgeLakeyHowWeWinAGuideToNonviolentDirectActionCampaig
ning2018MelvilleHousePublishing

CHAPTER SEVENTEEN

A BRAVE NEW WORLD

The globalist Empire wants a one world government with themselves as the hereditary monarchs. The rest of us will be reduced to mere feudal serfs without rights, identity, freewill or names; just cattle for the elites to do with as they wish. We are not going to allow this to happen.

One thing to consider is that the elites did not invent or create the idea of a one world government. They are right about a few things; we have to acknowledge that they are not stupid people; they are well-educated at the best universities with the best teachers the world has to offer.

"...the great question of our time is not whether or not one world can be achieved, but whether or not one world can be achieved by peaceful means. We shall have world government, whether or not we like it. The question is only whether world government will be achieved by consent or by conquest."

~ James John Warburg, February 17, 1950

Mr. Warburg was correct in his analysis. There will be a world government whether we like it or not. The real question for the common people is what kind of government will it be? A democratic, duly elected body with an international charter of rights that protects all the citizens of the world or a totalitarian nightmare ruled by sociopaths who destroy everything in their path?

Some evolutionary forces cannot be stopped: they can, however be delayed, managed, directed and controlled. The writing on the wall is clear that Earth will eventually progress to a world government. The elites are trying to shortcut the natural political evolution of our planet so they can be its rulers. They use revolutions, crisis, chaos and pandemics to achieve their goals. The more chaos they create, they more need there is for ORDER.

The quickest way to international peace is through international trade, international treaties, international schools, international conferences and many, many other international efforts that bring leaders together to discuss, negotiate, compromise and cooperate. Democracy is achieved when conflicting parties are brought to the negotiating table and resolutions and agreements are made.

There are already millions of people world-wide fighting these draconian, illegal lockdowns. United, we are a dragon, divided we are a pack of wild dogs. If we want to unleash the dragon on the Empire and destroy it to tiny bits, we MUST be united and organized in a massive global effort.

Horizontal Leadership

That doesn't mean we need a centralized organization. What we need is millions of independent cells that work in harmony yet act independently and autonomously. This style of offensive action is impossible to infiltrate and impossible to stop. And more importantly, millions of small independent groups can grow and become the seeds for an entirely new plan for global democracy. Obviously, what we have now isn't working.

The Empire has its plan for a Great Reset. We have to show the world a better plan, an even Greater Reset; a world where civil rights and freedoms are respected; a world without war. This isn't a pipe dream. This is going to happen. We will end this war and the entire system of banks, corporations and propaganda machines. That's our challenge and our mandate.

The reason why the Empire is collapsing is because it has no ideology that can unite people. It's a barren, empty tomb of greed, power, lust and war madness. The world can only be united by universal values of brotherhood, sisterhood, peace, love, tolerance and compassion. The world needs a spiritual love revolution. We've had a century of violent revolutions that have accomplished nothing except death and destruction.

It's time for the real revolution to begin. Long live the revolution!

CHAPTER EIGHTEEN

WHO ARE WE BEING?

We all know that we want to defeat this Empire of Greed but who are we being when we do this monumental task?

The truth is that some people don't know how to be a human being. Most people know how to be a doctor or a lawyer, soldier, sailor or candlestick maker but so many of us were never taught or just don't want to be a human being.

It's much easier to be a *human doing*. We are super animals with a big brain and opposable thumbs and that means we can make all kinds of cool stuff and think all kinds of smart things. We can ponder the cosmos and build cars, trains, automobiles and planes. Our cities are modern and marvelous; fast-paced, exciting and boundless with opportunities.

On the flip side the last one hundred years has produced a series of horrific wars; there were over 200 million deaths due to military conflict in the last century. Will this century be any different?

Our modern societies have millions of people who are good *human doings* but there is a shortage of good *human beings*. We don't have a plethora of spiritual leaders, teachers and social consultants to mirror our plethora of engineers, doctors, scientists and computer geeks. Most of our religious expression is based on ancient texts that although they still have much to offer and contain much inspiration that transcends the centuries, they also have much knowledge that is outdated, irrelevant and at odds with modern science.

Generally speaking, human doings are more successful in life than human beings. At least successful in terms of financial success, social status and quantity of possessions. Most of us in the West have a lot of stuff and we spend much quality time at the Stuffmart acquiring more stuff. There's nothing wrong with stuff and everyone likes cool stuff but if we aspire to be human beings we have to learn not to be preoccupied with the things of this world.

Generally speaking human beings aren't rewarded financially as well as human doings. And that's part of the secret of being a good human being. There's nothing in it for you. It's about the benefit of your actions to others.

> *"True beauty is born through our actions and aspirations and in the kindness we offer to others."*
>
> *~ Alek Wek*

You may never get any awards or receive a raise at work or make millions of dollars by being a good human being. You will make a lot of loyal friends though. A wise carpenter once said 2000 years ago, *What does it profit a man to win the world but lose his soul?* The answer is it doesn't. And the key word in this saying is *profit*. The difference between human doings and human beings is like the difference between *profits* and *prophets*.

The truth is we all need profits and prophets. We need to make a living and pay the rent and own a car. The love of money may be the root of all evil but poverty is a curse and we should either avoid it or if we are poor, we should work towards alleviating our poverty.

We also need prophets. We need people who have given it all up at some point in their lives in order to discover and become enlightened by the wisdom of their journey. Modern society is so overwhelming with all its attractions, distractions and contractions that there seems to be little time for enlightenment, meditation or communion with the great source and center.

The solution is actually pretty simple. It's all about motivation. We can have our busy lives and become better human beings in the process. We don't necessarily have to give up everything and go live in a monastery in the mountains. We just need a change of motivation from our preoccupation with *profit motive* and become centered around *service motive*.

> *"In life, it is never the big battle, the big moment, the big speech, the big election. That does not change things. What changes things is every day, getting up and rendering small acts of service and love beyond that what's expected of you or required of you."*
>
> *~ Cory Booker*

It's not an easy thing to walk away from the cares, comforts and rewards of busy modern life. Siddhartha Gautama, according to legend sat under a fig tree and discovered the mystery of human suffering. According to tradition, he was a wealthy man from a well-to-do family and he gave up all his possessions and his social position.

The good news is you don't need years of school and training to be a good human being. Anyone can do it no matter their race, sex, nationality or IQ—you just have to have a heart and have compassion for others. This is not hard to acquire because the vast majority of people already have these qualities, they just need to turn them on, like a switch. Kindness is a decision we make when presented with the opportunity.

The silver lining in the dark clouds hanging over the world is that the Empire has done the whole world a big favor by forcing us all to choose between a life of slavery to the techno-feudal Empire or a life of freedom, peace and brotherhood. We are all part of this global family connected to the great source and center of all creation. Everything we do affects everyone around us and though the world may be facing some very hard lessons, it is by our faith that we can continue to fight knowing the victory is already won.

Peace on Earth and Goodwill to All Human Beings

www.ingramcontent.com/pod-product-compliance
Lightning Source LLC
Chambersburg PA
CBHW061723250726

48657CB00002B/736